ABC's

OF CORN

By Lois F. Roets, Norma Kennebeck and Jean Marie Thelen

Illustrated by
María Angélica Guerrero

Hi there!

Thank you for purchasing this book! We hope you like it!!!!

We hope you learn about the wonderful corn plant and all it does for us from feeding our families to fueling our cars.

By purchasing this book you are making a contribution to the 4-H organization (www.4-H.org), an organization that has worked for over 100 years with over 100 public universities across the United States to bring leadership skills to millions of youth. 4-H is the largest youth development organization in North America.

Thanks again for purchasing this book and helping educate people on the value of corn!

Tony Thelen
Son of Jean Marie Thelen
June 2024

Original quilt art from Shirley Neary, daughter of Jean Marie Thelen

Acknowledgments

There are so many people who contributed to this book over the years. At the risk of missing someone, I want to acknowledge all who supported making this book a reality.

First the many family members who contributed historical articles and/or ideas: Ron Schelle, Shirley Neary, Joyce Sieve, Jalynn Wanninger, Doreen Schelle Sandberg, Karen Thelen-Phillips, Ed Thelen, Diane Rosenthal, Barb Kidney, Linda Johnston, Becky Schelle Evans, Marilyn Underberg, Phyllis Lawler, Virginia Kennebeck, Julie Kennebeck Nixon, Denny Kennebeck, Judy Tiefenthaler, Laurie McCallum, Gayle F. Bortz, Mike Schelle, KB Kennebeck, Nicole Schelle Sammons-Houser, Sheila Thelen, and Andy Kennebeck.

The project was originally drafted as a manuscript with no illustrations. The outstanding color illustrations were provided by Maria Angelica Guerrero.

Finally, in the ultimate acknowledgement of all, is the life and times of the three authors - Lois Roets, Norma Kennebeck, and Jean Marie Thelen. These three women had the original vision and were the catalyst to make this book a reality. May they rest in peace knowing that their lives mattered not only to their families, but they also created a way to contribute to the lives of others through the pages of this book.

A is for agriculture, the
Art of farming
And cultivating the soil.
Acres of corn growing tall.
All will be food for
Animals and people
After harvest in the fall.
April plantings of
Acres of corn, grow
A lot of green corn that becomes
Ablaze with golden stalks, ready for
Autumn harvest.
AWESOME SIGHT.

CORN FACT An ear of corn averages 800 kernels in 16 rows.

Q&A

QUESTION: Which is bigger: an acre of corn or a football field?

ANSWER: They are about the same. An acre is 160 square rods or 4840 square yards. That's the size of a football field from one goal line to just inside the 10 yard line at the other end.

FIELD RESEARCH

In late spring or early summer, locate a field with growing corn.

Observe the field three different times to watch it grow.
Record your observations: date, description, sketch of what you saw.

Date	Description	Sketch of what you saw

Date	Description	Sketch of what you saw

Bushels of dried corn
Become
Bags of popcorn for people.
Buckets of corn
Become feed for pigs, chickens, and
Beef cattle so they grow
Big and healthy

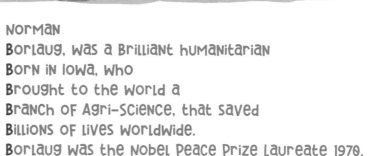

Norman
Borlaug, was a brilliant humanitarian
Born in Iowa, who
Brought to the world a
Branch of Agri-Science, that saved
Billions of lives worldwide.
Borlaug was the Nobel Peace Prize Laureate 1970.

INTERNET RESEARCH   How did Borlaug save lives?

CORN FACT   Corn proteins are unable to combine with yeast to make leavened bread. That's why cornbread is thicker and will not rise like the breads of other grains.

FIELD RESEARCH   Compare corn flakes and another corn cereal.
Compare 3 factors: shape, taste, nutrition value.

	Corn Flakes	Other Corn Cereal
Shape		
Taste		
Nutritional Value		

The whole corn plant is used; nothing is wasted.

Corn to eat:
Cornbread
Corn Chips
Corn Flakes
Corn dogs. YUM!

Corn to use:
Corncob pipe
Cobs for kindling,
Corn husks for bedding.
Corn cribs store corn.

CORN FACT

"Corn Belt" states of Iowa, Illinois, Nebraska and Minnesota account for over 50% of corn grown in United States according to a 2010 report.

INTERNET RESEARCH

Look up picture of a corn crib on the internet. Corn cribs are structures that hold corn. Air flows through open spaces and the corn dries. Why? Drying the corn prevents mold.

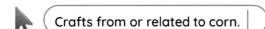

Crafts from or related to corn.

What is a "cover crop?"

Crayons are made with cornstarch. How is this done?

FUN FACT

Corn varieties grow from two to twenty feet high. Stalks have eight to 48 leaves and produce one or multiple ears.

Doors can be
Decorated with ears of corn and ribbon.
Designs of corn
Decorate clothes, blankets and
Dishes.

South Dakota's Corn Palace is decorated with corn scenes – a dynamic example of using corn for decoration.

Dangers to corn plant
During corn growing season may be
Deadly hailstorms that can
Demolish a corn crop, or
Dynamic winds that break the stalk and
Cut off its food supply from the roots.

Q&A

QUESTION: What is Dent Corn?

ANSWER: Dent is a variety of corn that, when dry, has a dip or dent at the tip of each kernel. It is also called field corn. Dent corn is used for cornmeal flour, corn chips and taco shells.

EQUIPMENT

Corn Dryer is a machine that produces heat which flows through corn to lower the moisture of the corn seed

INTERNET RESEARCH

What other equipment and machines are used in growing corn?

CORN FACT

"Dry-milling" a bushel of corn will produce
• 10 one-pound boxes of cereal and
• 15 pounds of brewers grits (enough for one gallon of beer) and
• 10 eight-ounce packages of cheese curls and
• 1 pound of pancake or other mix and
• 22 pounds of hominy feed for livestock and
• .7 pounds of corn oil. (The Carroll Herald. Jan. 28, 1997)

Ears of corn show
Even rows from
Eight to 22

Energy from the sun helps corn grow.

CORN FACT Embryo or germ of a corn kernel contains most of the fat, vitamins and minerals in corn. For a seed to germinate, grow, it must contain a living embryo that stays alive 3-5 years. If kept in cool dry storage, corn seeds can live 25 years or more.

Elevators help move corn from one place to another.
Elevators have "shelves" linked together
with a chain with space between the
shelves. The motor pulls the
chains and that moves
the shelves of corn
along a path to
where corn
needs to
be.

Draw an elevator of your own!

INTERNET RESEARCH What does a "corn snake" look like?

YOUR OPINION Do you like popcorn balls?

FUN FACT Corn varieties grow from two to twenty feet high. Stalks have eight to 48 leaves and produce one or multiple ears.

How to enjoy
Fresh corn-on-the cob:
Buy Fresh corn at the grocery store or roadside stand.
Free the ear of husks, silks,
Boil in water or roast on grill. Add
Fresh herbs, butter, salt and pepper, and enjoy.

YOUR OPINION What seasonings do you like on sweet corn?

Fuel from Corn: Ethanol
Corn can be converted to ethanol fuel to run motors.

INTERNET RESEARCH How is ethanol made?

YOUR OPINION Do you use ethanol in your car? Give reasons for your choice.

CORN FACT Flint Corn has a smooth kernel with no soft starch in the endosperm. It ranges in color from white to deep red. Flint corn grows well in high altitudes, cool climate and wet soils.

Corn cobs can be burned as fuel for warmth. Dried cobs are good kindling.

Haiku poetry has 3 lines: 5 syllables in first, 7 syllables in second, 5 syllables in third line.

Example of a corn Haiku

Silent corn cobs wait
For a match to light a fire
To warm a cold night.

Your Haiku

Topic: _____

(5 Syllables) _____

(7 Syllables) _____

(5 Syllables) _____

FUN FACT Corn cobs make good corks (stoppers).

To grow, corn needs:
Fertile ground (soil),
healthy seeds,
appropriate moisture,
warm sunshine,
proper cultivation,
time to grow to maturity.

When you harvest corn leave some kernels to feed,
and stalks to protect, wildlife during winter's cold and storms.

CORN COUNTS

A pound of corn has approximately 1300 kernels.

Today, a single U.S. farmer provided food and fiber for 155 people according to the U.S. Department of Agriculture

Genes and Genetics

Gene: basic unit of heredity.
Genetic: relating to genes
Genetics: the scientific study of genes and heredity.

Two scientists worthy of study:
Gregor Mendel (1822-1884) established basic rules of genetics and heredity through cross pollinating plants and recording what grew.
Barbara McClintock (1902-1992) discovered that some genes do not behave as predicted but they transpose, jump over, regular patterns of heredity.

DEFINITION

Gluten is a sticky protein substance found in corn and other grains.

INTERNET RESEARCH

Why do some people avoid eating gluten?

FIELD RESEARCH

Purchase or bake "regular" and gluten free bread.
What differences do you see and taste? Other comparisons?

HAVE YOU NOTICED?

Grocery stores now have many choices for gluten-free products

 yes   Not Yet

CORN FACT

In batteries, cornstarch is often used as an electrical conductor

FUN FACT

Glue on envelopes is made of cornstarch that becomes sticky when moistened.

Heaps of
Heavenly popcorn keep you
Healthy and
Happy.

YOUR OPINION Do you prefer "plain" popcorn or seasoned popcorn?

Hybrid: a plant formed by cross-pollinating two select plants.
Plant Botany: The tassel is the male part of the corn plant. The ear is the female part.

For corn kernels to develop, the pollen of the tassel must fertilize the silks of the corn ear.
For every single grain of pollen that follows a silk to the corn ear, a kernel of corn can grow.
For most corn, wind blows the pollen and the silks capture the pollen grains.

Some characteristics for which corn hybrids are developed:
- disease resistant - sturdiness of stalk to resist wind and hold ears.
- length of growing season, - length of ear so more kernels are produced

Q&A

QUESTION: Can I create a hybrid corn plant?

ANSWER: Yes. To create a hybrid, the pollen of one selected plant is used to fertilize the silks of another selected plant. To control pollination of the silks, the tassel of the plant is removed so that no pollen falls on its own silks. This is called "detasseling." In test plots, the silks are covered to keep out pollen from itself, To "cross/hybrid" the plant, the selected tassel is shook over the silks, several times over a few days. This cross pollination creates hybrid corn that carries the genes of both plants.

Corn is harvested. when it is just right for the intended use of the corn.

"Just right" for drying as seed means kernels are hard and moisture is just enough to keep the germ alive but not too much moisture that the seed will rot.

"Just right" for human consumption means shells on kernels are soft and juicy.

YOUR OPINION

"Cornucopia" represents overflowing abundance.

Draw a cornucopia. What "fullness and abundance" is in your cornucopia?

CORN FACT Corn is produced on every continent of the world with exception of Antarctica.

FUN FACT The number of leaves in the husk is a direct result of the number of joints in the corn stalk.

Iowa's rolling hills and flat floodplains grow lots and lots of corn.

Iowa's fertile land was formed by the Ice Age and rivers, and wisely used by Insightful farmers who Industriously farm the gift of land.

Iowa State University (ISU) in Ames provides information, research, test plots on growing corn.

Q&A

QUESTION: What is "Indian corn"?

ANSWER: Corn with colored kernels. It can be eaten and is often used for decorations.

INTERNET RESEARCH   Recipes for "Indian Corn Pudding" and "Indian Corn Bread."

FIELD RESEARCH   Visit a processing plant that cans or freezes corn.

Q&A

QUESTION: What is "Immature corn"?

ANSWER: Corn that is not fully grown (matured) for its intended use.

FIELD RESEARCH   How many styles of corn can you find at a grocery store? List the name and description of each (examples: whole corn, creamed corn…)

_____

_____

_____

CORN FACT   Plastics made from corn are less expensive than those made from oil.

Q&A

QUESTION: : What happens when you add cornstarch to hot liquid, like gravy?

ANSWER: Ask a cook. Watch the cook add cornstarch to a hot liquid.

FUN FACT

Corn grows well in Iowa because:
• growing season is long and warm enough for corn.
• rainfall is usually enough.
• soil is fertile and deep.
• farmers know how to grow and harvest corn.

Johnny cake is made from corn and other baking ingredients.

Jelly beans are NOT made from corn but can be made to taste like popcorn.
July in Iowa brings hot days and slightly cooler nights – ideal for corn growing.
Jelly from corn cobs (white or red) is made from, you guessed it, corn cobs.

  **INTERNET RESEARCH**   How many recipes for corn cob jelly can you find?

 FIELD RESEARCH   Visit specialty markets to find a jar of corn cob jelly.
Do you like it? What does it taste like? If you couldn't find corn cob jelly, match a batch of corn cob jelly.

INTERNET RESEARCH   " Paintings of Corn Fields by Grant Wood"

Enjoy the paintings of Iowa's artist, Grant Wood.
What do you see? Can you sketch one of his drawings?

 HAVE YOU NOTICED?   The rolling hills on the landscape of Iowa? Iowa is not flat except on some floodplains*.   yes   Not Yet

 DEFINE   What does a "floodplain" look like? Describe or draw it.

 CORN FACT   Cornstarch is a common ingredient in cosmetic and hygiene items.

Kk

kernels on cobs,
kernels stuck in our teeth,
kernels your body will eat and convert into energy and endurance.

INTERNET RESEARCH Find a picture of a cross-section of a corn kernel

Draw it and label 3 parts:

- Endosperm
- Pericarp
- Germ

CORN FACT The ear located closest to the top of the stalk becomes the largest ear

INTERNET RESEARCH Illustrate the difference between a corn stalk and a corm.

Corn Stalk	Corm

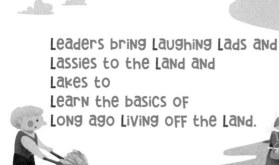

Leaders bring Laughing Lads and
Lassies to the Land and
Lakes to
Learn the basics of
Long ago Living off the Land.

 YOUR IDEA   What does "living off the land" mean?

 If you had to "live off the land" like the pioneers did, what 21 items would you like to take with you?

Compare your list with lists of others.

1	2	3
4	5	6
7	8	9
10	11	12
13	14	15
16	17	18
19	20	21

 **INTERNET RESEARCH**   What does "Corn Rows" hairdo look like?

 CORN FACT   Sweet corn syrup is a main ingredient in cough drops and hard candies

Maize Mazes can be fun,
Making your way through
Marked paths,
Making wrong turns, but finally
Mastering the corn field puzzle.
Maize is another name for corn.
Maze is a pathway puzzle you enter and find your way to the end.
Caution: Don't go into a maze alone. Have a cell phone with you.

YOUR IDEA

Design a corn maze.

Corn Science

Corn is a **monocotyledon**.
A **cotyledon** is the first leaf grown from a seed. "Mono" means one. Corn plants sprout with one (mono) leaf and produce a single stalk and one tap root.

YOUR RESEARCH

Loosely roll corn kernels and beans in a moist towel. Keep the roll warm and damp until seeds sprout.
Corn kernels will have single sprouts (monocotyledons.)
Beans will have a double sprout because beans are dicotyledons.

Notice how the sprouts go towards the water or wet part of the towel. What else did you see?

Q&A

Question: What is the "milk stage" of an ear of corn?

Answer: Corn has a milk stage before the kernels harden or dry. Cream corn includes much of the milk of young corn.

CORN USE

Corn pellet stoves are used for heating.

What do "corn pellets" look like? How are they made?

November gray skies,
Nippy winds
Nudge us to finish harvest of corn and root vegetables.

Q&A

QUESTION: Are you a "nosher?" To "nosh" means to eat or nibble at food. If you are a "nosher" you like to nibble and eat.

ANSWER: only you know the answer to this question!

FIELD RESEARCH What foods for noshing are made of corn? Read the labels.

INTERNET RESEARCH What is the nutrition value of your favorite corn?

Which state is called the Cornhusker state? Why?

HAVE YOU NOTICED? Look at the skies in November. Write or draw a description of "November skies" 3 days in a row, at about the same time of day.

November Skies   Time:

Day 1	Day 2	Day 3

CORN FACT The root system of a healthy corn plant grows into the soil 5 or more feet until it reaches the water table.

Oil from corn tastes good so it is used in foods, salads, stews, and dressings.

Compare the taste of corn oil and other oils.

Organic corn is corn raised without use of pesticides or fertilizers.
Some people think organic corn is healthier to eat.
Some people think organic corn is more subject to disease since no pesticides are used.

 INTERNET RESEARCH Read about organic foods. Learn what organic means.

 RESEARCH Listen to the opinions of others.

 YOUR OPINION What do you believe about organic foods? Based on your opinion, which foods do you prefer to eat?

 HAVE YOU NOTICED? Can you tell the difference between regular corn and organic corn just by looking at it? yes / Not yet

 YOUR RESEARCH Prepare organic and regular sweet corn in the same way. Can you taste the difference?

INTERNET RESEARCH In 2007, Iowa corn growers averaged 182 bushels per acre. What was the average number of bushels, per acre, in these years?

Year/Bushels per acre

Year	Bushels per acre	Year	Bushels per acre
2007	182		
2008		2015	
2009		2016	
2010		2017	
2011		2018	
2012		2019	
2013		2020	
2014		2021	

What is a "corny" joke? Do you know corny jokes? Share them with friends.

 OPINION POLL Conduct an opinion poll using kernels of corn. Display the question and provide a jar for each choice. Participants "vote" by dropping one kernel of corn into the jar of choice. What did you learn by doing a "Kernel Poll?"

POP - POP - POP
Popping
Popcorn on the
Porch for
Parade of players,
Parents and
Pets at the Park.

Playful
Poems about
People
Pets
Pickles and
Puzzles
Promises a
Pleasant
Program [performance].

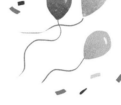

Corn Science

Pollen from the tassel falls on the silks and travels to the ear. This is pollination. When pollination takes place, corn kernels can grow.

FIELD RESEARCH

Plant a few corn seeds in spring. Watch the plant grow, produce tassels and silks, and watch the breezes blow pollen to the silks. Then, when the ears of corn are just right, pick and cook the corn, then eat! What did you learn by doing this research?

CORN FACT

Popcorn pops because heat causes the starch and moisture in the endosperm to expand and "pop" out of its hard flint kernel coat.

INTERNET RESEARCH

Is a "peppercorn" a corn product?

QUESTION

If you or your achievement is described as a "corker," are you being praised or criticized?

Corn plants
Quiver and
Quake in summer prairie breezes.

Quick-freeze is a method of preserving corn to retain its freshness and taste at the peak of harvest.

 INTERNET RESEARCH What does the Corn Row quilt pattern look like?

 YOUR IDEA Can YOU design a quilt block using the corn theme? Sketch and color your newly-designed quilt block. What will you call your Corn Block design?

 YOUR OPINION "In the Quiet of the night, you can hear the corn grow." Is this true? Not true? If true, what makes the "growing sound?"

Haiku poetry has 3 lines: 5 syllables in first, 7 syllables in second, 5 syllables in third line.

Haiku on Drones

High above drones fly
To see buildings, fields, livestock.
Drones help farmers farm.

Your Haiku

Topic: _____

(5 Syllables) _____

(7 Syllables) _____

(5 Syllables) _____

Radiate joy when you
Reminisce memories of corn. Raise your hands and clap.
Recognize the multiple use of corn.
Regard farmers with honor. Learn from them.
Regale good cooks. Will they share their recipes?
Relax while you eat.
Rejoice that corn is a part of way of your life.

 FIELD RESEARCH

How many places did you see corn at the State or County Fair? Don't forget the food stands that use corn or corn meal in preparing the food.

 INTERNET RESEARCH

Do a search for "corn recipes" on Internet.

Study Index to see how many recipes for corn are in a cook book. Use several cook books.

 FIELD RESEARCH

Ask relatives to see their recipes that use corn.
Do they use a "written down" recipe or cook by memory, look and touch?

 YOUR IDEA

Create your own recipe that uses corn.

 YOUR OPINION

What is your favorite way to eat corn?

Watch how fast corn grows in warm sunshine!

 CORN FACT

Corn has one tap or main root that holds the plant in place.
As the corn stalk grows, the plant grows "threads" that grow into the soil to help the tap root anchor the plant.

Corn is consumed as a vegetable and as
   Starch in foods,
   Syrup and sweeteners,
   Snack foods, like corn chips.

Grocery
   Shelves are
   Stocked with
   Salsa.

DEFINITION Salsa: a mixture of vegetables and seasonings added to sandwich, meat or fish dish, or eaten with chips or crackers.

INTERNET RESEARCH How many recipes for corn salsa can you find?

YOUR OPINION Your favorite salsa?

FIELD RESEARCH How many varieties of SALSA does your local grocery store have?

YOUR IDEA Pretend you have developed hybrid seed corn.
Design a seed sack for your hybrids.
Or, create an original corn salsa recipe and design a label for it.

INTERNET RESEARCH What is a corn shock? What was its purpose?

Safety in the Field

If you get lost, follow one row until you come to the end of the row. Stand or sit outside the corn where you are visible. Call for help.

DO NOT go back into the field.

Tassels produce pollen,
Then release it
To land on the silks.
Then kernels develop on the ears.

An A"maize"ingly
Tasty Treat That Tickles
Taste buds of
Theatre patrons [POPCORN]

 YOUR IDEA How would you illustrate or describe " popcorn tickling your taste buds?"

 INTERNET RESEARCH   There are many Testings and Tastings in growing corn. How many can you list or describe?

 YOUR OPINION   Does a hamburger made of "organic" beef taste better or different than a hamburger of "regular" beef?

 FUN FACT   Corn descended from a plant called teosinte that still grows in Mexico.

UNder the GROUND,
UNder the WatchFUL eye OF Mother Nature,
UNSeeN, a CORN kerNel SprOUts, aNd SeNdS UP a
ShOOt that GROWS

UP,
UP,
UP, to becOme a very tall
Stalk, ready tO prOdUce cOrN.

CORN leaveS
    UNFOld aNd
    UNFURl tO create aN
    Umbrella FOR wildlife.

YOUR IDEA Write a story of life that lives under the umbrella created by corn leaves.

INTERNET RESEARCH Regular corn grows in one season. Is there a "perennial" corn plant that grows more than one season?

HAVE YOU NOTICED? The color of corn leaves varies because of type of corn, amount of water and sunlight the plant receives, and stages of growing season.

Other things you noticed?

FUN FACT First known ears of corn were tiny, only a few inches long.

Village schools shut down for
Vacation [corn picking] time is here again.
Vital to the harvesting of corn as vast majority of kids help out with vim and
Vigor and fun to gather
Varieties of corn in the fields for
Very happy farmers to fill the corn cribs.

DEFINITION

Corn Picking Vacation. This was 1-2 weeks out of school to help pick corn. Corn was hand-picked from the stalks before there were machines to pick it. Also, if there had been a powerful wind, corn would have fallen to the ground. This corn needed to be picked up - as much as was possible.

CORN FACT   Corn is rich in Vitamin C.

INTERNET RESEARCH   Corn has been found at archeological sites 7000 years ago. Do all sources agree, or do sources suggest other timelines?

YOUR IDEA   How would you organize a "Corn Festival" for your community?

Guidelines

- Some activities for many ages
- Safety of activities
- Budget for supplies and prizes
- Prizes and recognitions
- Hold interest of participants and on-lookers
- Date and times
- Location
- Will you have music?
- Will there be a Master of Ceremonies?
- Other plans??

Henry A.
Wallace, Former Secretary of Agriculture, knew
Weather and
Wind were important
When growing corn, and
Weeds had to be controlled.

Harvest time:
Waiting is over,
Wagons hitched up [horses], Walking beside at a brisk pace – Wasting no time,
Wearing gloves with hooks or pegs each in their own
Way of picking corn,
Whamming the corn ears on the bang boards of the wagon .

Old Days

Description of picking corn by hand using wagons with "bang boards."

Wagons were used to bring in the corn. These wagons or pickups had a bed or box as standard equipment. Then "bang boards" were added. These were 3 or 4 boards nailed together to create a panel that could be attached to one side of the wagon. Extension to one side of wagon or truck was called a "bang board" because, when corn was picked by hand, the person would twist the ear of corn from the stalk, then toss it into the wagon. If the picker tossed too hard or high, the ear of corn could go over the top and fall into the field. If the ear hit the bang board, it would fall into the wagon. The ear of corn made a "bang" when it hit the bang board extension.

Interview someone who picked corn by hand. How was the process described?

CORN FACT

"Wet-milling" a bushel of corn will produce
• 31.5 pounds of starch or 33 pounds of sweetener or
• 2.5 gallons of fuel ethanol and
• 10.9 pound of 21% protein food and
• 2.6 pounds of 60% gluten meal and
• 16 pounds of corn oil. (The Carroll Herald. Jan. 28, 1997)

INTERNET RESEARCH

Can you make alcohol from corn?

I'M **ex**cited about corn so I
express
exuberance for the
extra good
exhilarating taste of first corn of the season.

DEFINITION

Xenia refers to transfer of pollen from one variety of plant to endosperm of another variety, resulting in hybrid characteristics.

Xylem the woody tissue of a plant that permits water and minerals to move within the plant.

INTERNET RESEARCH

What is "xanthan gum?"

Exports are critical to American agriculture.
What agricultural products does the United States e**X**port?

Products	Sold to these countries

CORN FACT   Explosives may contain corn products.

YOU

YOU COME FROM STRONG PEOPLE,
YOU LOVE YOUR FAMILY AND THEY LOVE YOU.
YOU TAKE EACH DAY AND USE IT WISELY.
    THIS LEAVES A LEGACY – EACH DAY.
        WHAT OF YOUR EFFORTS TODAY WILL BENEFIT TOMORROW?

YOU ARE ONE CYCLE AMONG MANY CYCLES.
YOU ARE OF THIS
    YEAR, ALL
    YESTERYEARS AND
    YEARS TO COME.
YOU WILL LIVE IN MEMORY YEARS AFTER YOU DIE.

YOU ARE IMPORTANT.
YOU ARE, AND CONTRIBUTE, TO THE WORLD AS NO OTHER CAN.
    LIFE HAS CYCLES WITHIN CYCLES.

My Memory

Every year I need to see and feel the fall harvest. I remember and re-live good memories growing up on a farm that raised hybrid seed corn and other living things.

YOUR IDEA

Write or recall a childhood memory?

INTERNET RESEARCH

Yield is the amount of corn grown on an acre of ground. Why does yield change with each growing season?

FUN FACT

Yogurt may use corn syrup to sweeten it. Corn starch gives yogurt and ice cream a consistent texture.

Zz

ZOOM iN,
Look Closely,
Live respectfully, With nature.

 DEFINITION

Growing **zones** tell us which plants will do well in which parts of the world. Different seeds grow well in different growing zones.

Feel the zephyrs, Which blow Continuously in iowa,
– assuring us of another day and another season.

 YOUR IDEA

Write a poem about zephyrs blowing on prairies.

🔍 **ZOOM** in on a corn kernel or cob with a magnifying glass or microscope.

Write or draw what you see.

 ADD CORN FACTS

What facts about corn should be added to this booklet?

The author's father, Charles G. Schelle, produced hybrid corn seeds in the 1940-1960. Below is a copy of the company stationary.

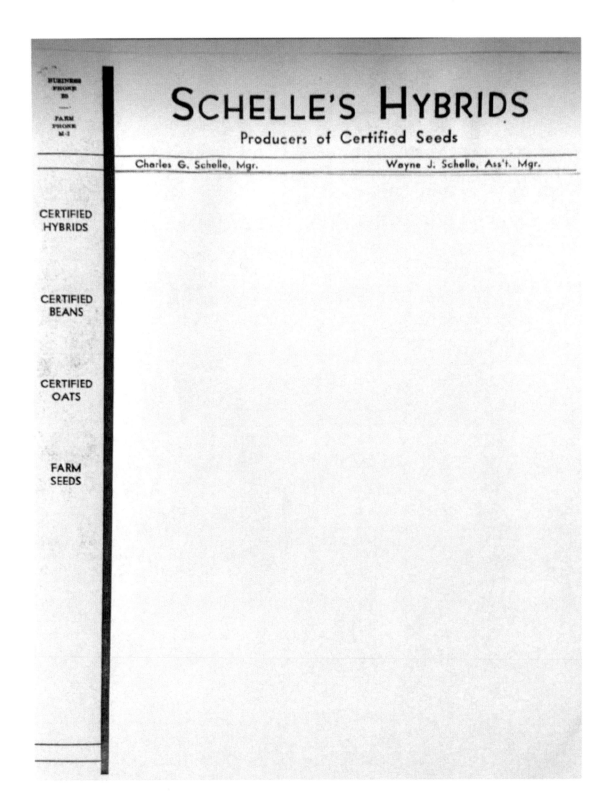

Schelle Family Farm History

The Author's Upbringing on an American Farm

The three authors of this book grew up on a family farm in western Iowa in the 20th century. Their parents, Charles and Mary Schelle, raised a family of 8 on a 160 acre farm west of Breda, Iowa.

The "corn belt" is a geographic location of the United States particularly suited to growing corn. Breda, Iowa, is located in the middle of the corn belt, right where the "n" is in the word "Corn" in the map.

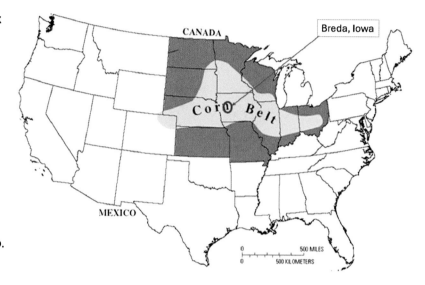

Figure 1 An early family photo with authors Norma Kennebeck (first row left side), Jean Marie Thelen (2nd row left side), and Lois Roets (2nd row right side)

Figure 2 Above is an original photo of the author's family farmstead, followed by another photo describing what each building was on the farm.

ABC's of Corn ©2024 Lois Roets, Norma Kennebeck, & Jean Marie Thelen

The authors did many jobs on the farm, including:

- Gathering eggs every morning
- Milking Cows
- Weeding the Garden
- Repairing fences
- Picking and Canning fruit and other food for the winter
- Mending clothes and fixing equipment
- Detasseling corn in the summer months
- Cleaning and maintaining equipment
- Assisting with cooking and household chores

While they did these jobs they learned many values:

- Hard Work Ethic
- Self-Reliance
- Stewardship of the Land
- Resilience and Adaptability
- Community and Cooperation
- Frugality and Resourcefulness
- Commitment and Responsibility
- Respect for Animals

Figure 3 A typical corn detasseling team in the 1940's. Author Norma Kenenebeck is in the front row, first on the right. Wayne Schelle, her brother, is also in the front row, sitting first on the left. These crews removed the "tassel" from the corn plans so that pollen from the neighboring rows could pass along favorable corn traits to future seeds

All of the Schelle kids had 4-H projects as children that related to learning the operations of a farm and running a successful business.

Figure 4 Two of the authors in their new 4-H uniforms. Jean Marie Thelen is back row second from the left, and Lois Roets is back row second from the right.

The authors not only did all of these jobs, but their father Charles also ran a business developing hybrid corn seeds from 1940 – 1960. Schelle Hybrid Corn Seeds was early in the green revolution to optimize adapting corn genetics to higher yields.

Figure 5 The delivery truck driven by Wayne Schelle, brother of the authors.
As provided by Ron Schelle, brother of the authors.

It all started in the late 1930's when Charles and his family picked corn by hand in the field. A wagon was pulled along by a couple of horses named Dick and June in the field. The Schelle family would strip the ear of corn off the plant and toss it against a "bank board" on the wagon. However, every once in a while, they saw a good ear of corn and they would set it aside in a special box. The box was emptied at noon and end of the day. The ears of corn from the "special box" with perfect seed traits would then be used to breed better seeds for the future.

When the seeds from these special ears of corn were planted they had bags placed over the tassels and silk during pollination season. The pollen was shaken off the 1 plant and placed in the bag covering the silk of another plant. This "inbreeding" enabled Charles Schelle to develop high yielding corn hybrids for local farmers.

Fast Facts:

- It took 6-8 years to produce a successful hybrid corn seed variety.
- The author's father sold a 52 lb. bag of seed for $6-8 to local farmers in the 1940's
- Today, bags of seed cost between $200-300/bag

By selectively breeding plants that produced a high yield, their father was able to create seeds that he sold to other farmers to improve their yield. The seeds These seeds over the years enabled farmers to grow yield from ~ 150 bushels per acre to over 300 bushels per acre. These seeds, along with modern farming techniques, have helped to feed, clothe, and fuel a growing world!!!

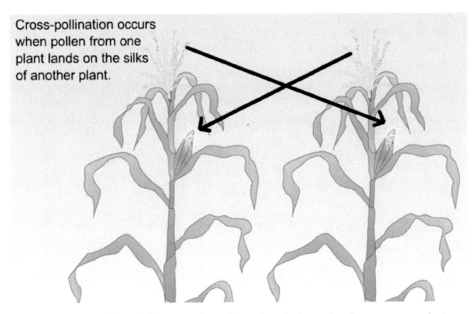

Cross-pollination occurs when pollen from one plant lands on the silks of another plant.

Figure 6 A good visual of how seed corn is produced - the pollen from one corn plant falls on the silky ears of another. As provided by Ron Schelle, brother of the authors.

Once the corn matured and was ready for harvest, the corn was hand-picked and taken to a seed corn processing facility. The corn was dried "upstairs" where heat would rise and dry the seeds faster. Once dried, the seeds were hand-shucked, graded (keep only the flat seeds, and toss out the round ones at each end of the ear of corn). From there, they were packaged in burlap Schelle Seed Corn bags (see Fig. 7)

Figure 7 An original Schelle Hybrid burlap seed corn bag from ~ 1956 as provided by the author's nephew Mike Schelle

Figure 8 A typical social scene from the early 1950's. In this case, a group of men gathered to celebrate the wedding of author Jean Marie Thelen in 1951.

Schelle Hybrids and Boystown of Omaha, Nebraska

At one point, in 1944, the author's father donated 5 bushels of his best hybrid seed to Boys Town in Omaha, Nebraska. See the photo in Fig 1 below of the author's brother, Wayne, visiting with Father Flanagan, the founder of Boys Town.

Figure 9 Fr. Flanagan, Founder of Boys Town in Omaha, NE, with Wayne Schelle, the author's brother, in 1944. The year this picture was taken Charles Schelle donated 5 bushels of his highest yielding seeds to Boys Town. Photo provided by Judy Tiefenthaler and Jaylynn Wanniger daughters of Wayne Shelle, the author's brother and COO of Schelle Hybrid

SCHELLE'S HYBRIDS
Producers of Certified Seeds

Charles G. Schelle, Mgr.   Wayne J. Schelle, Ass't. Mgr.

BREDA, IOWA
August 21, 1944

CERTIFIED
HYBRIDS

CERTIFIED
BEANS

CERTIFIED
OATS

FARM
SEEDS

The Reverend That

Realizing the working you are doing in an effort to lead homeless boys toward heavenly shores, I am asking you to accept a donation from me. As a producer of hybrid seed corn and other farm seeds we are offering to you as a donation 5 bu. of our best and highest yielding state certified hybrid seed corn for your territory. Or if you have your seed corn spoken for, may I offer you 10 bu. of State Certified Richland for 25 bu. of uncertified Tama Oats.

Please accept this as a token of our appreciation for the work you are doing. I realize it is not very much but we hope every little bit will count.

Waiting to hear from you and praying that God may be with you to continue your splendid work, I remain.

Respectfully Yours,

Our Aim Is To Please Our Customers

Figure 10 The 1944 letter to Father Flanagan written by the author's brother, Wayne Schelle.

Schelle Hybrid Seed Co Promotional Materials

Figure 11 A Schelle Hybrid rain bonnet still in its case from ~ 1945 provided by author Norma Kennebeck's daughter Marilyn Underberg

Figure 12 A Schelle Hybrid salt and pepper shaker from ~1945 provided by Karen Thelen-Phillips, daughter of author Jean Marie Thelen

Figure 13 A thermometer promotional item as shared by Ed Thelen, son of Jean Marie Thelen

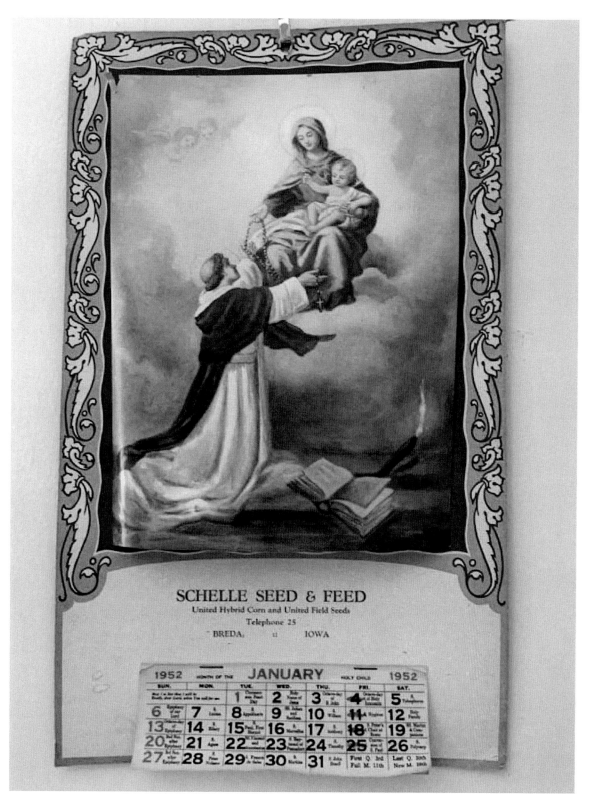

Figure 14 A calendar from 1952 promoting Schelle Hybrids. The picture is called "The Presentation of the Rosary". It demonstrates the Catholic identity of the Schelle Seed Corn business and the Breda, Iowa, Community. If you look closely, the telephone number to call the business was "25" – back then phones were much simpler!!!!! Calendar provided by Diane Rosenthal, daughter of Bill Schelle, brother of the authors

Figure 15 (above and below) A mirror promoting Schelle Hybrid Seed Corn (above) and a close up of the slogans (below). Provided by the author's brother Ron Schelle.

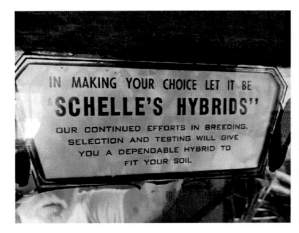

Figure 16 The actual Schelle Family Farm with all buildings named. Location was 2.5 miles west of Breda, Iowa. Note the Hog Barnk & Chicken Coop. The family also raised cattle - all fed with grain raised on the farm. As provided by Ron Schelle, brother of the authors

Figure 17 A family photo with authors Jean Marie Thelen (first row, left side), Norma Kennebeck (first row right side), and Lois Roets (2nd row, 3rd from the left)

Made in the USA
Monee, IL
07 September 2024

65331473R00029